SKEENA

Caitlin Press Inc.
3375 Ponderosa Way,
Qualicum Beach, BC V9K 2J8
www.caitlin-press.com

Edited by Patricia Young
Text design by Vici Johnstone
Cover design by Briar Craig
Printed in Canada

Caitlin Press Inc. acknowledges financial support from the Government of Canada and the Canada Council for the Arts, and from the Province of British Columbia through the British Columbia Arts Council and the Book Publisher's Tax Credit.
Library and Archives Canada Cataloguing in Publication

de Leeuw, Sarah, author

  Skeena / Sarah de Leeuw.

Poems.

ISBN 978-1-927575-91-8 (paperback)

  I. Title.

PS8607.E2352S54 2015   C811'.6   C2015-904043-4

SKEENA

Sarah de Leeuw

CAITLIN PRESS

More Praise for Skeena

"In *Skeena*, the long poem surges into history, cracks open geology, pushes time itself, maps the length of a river's habitat into language. Tender and delicate, this poem also pulses with energy visceral enough to perform an extraordinary feat: river as persona flows diaphanous, syllables investigating a complicated and contested space. Ethereal yet concrete enough to hold place names, landscape descriptions, paeans to moon, wolf, and salmon, conversations with that most destructive life form, humankind. This is a North Country epic: join the journey de Leeuw creates: a book-length water-saga, uncontainable, a force calling: come, let me take you—"

—Renée Saklikar

"*Skeena* is a poem/assemblage of intelligence and care that contains an epic sweep of northern history, geography, and the landscape of human experience therein. It is a large determined document in and of place 'that finds out.' The prehistoric, the fauna, the flora, all that inhabits it—and the forces that threaten this complex—is what this writing reveals. Herein the Skeena, the river—words that move to give a new and important sense of our bearings."

—Barry McKinnon

Skeena is dedicated to the memory of my father.
Dionys de Leeuw introduced me to and taught me to love the Skeena River.
He is now with the Skeena River.

This poem is, to borrow the words of Alice Oswald (2002), "made from" many different descriptions, representations, voices, images, and contemplations of the Skeena River. *Skeena* stiches together entries from — to name a few — historical newspapers, highway signs, First Nations band newsletters, tourist websites, local testimonials, museum chronicles, stories, and scientific reports. I have translated and adapted these multiple archives to construct a poetic rendering of the Skeena River — into which I have written the river's voice. The Skeena River is British Columbia's second-largest river contained entirely in the province. The river is situated wholly in the province's northern regions, traversing traditional and contemporary territories of six First Nations.

Prince Rupert City & Regional Archives, J. D. Allen photo; P991-70-6116.

Skeena Crossing

What is this   this crossing?

In the photo   just in front of the train with the crane at the edge of the   drop
                                off from track into river
           stands a young man.

        Truss truss.   From left.
        Truss truss.   From right.
        A bridge   built   middleward.
                    Inward.

Bridge — bridge — bridge — bridge — water. Bridge — bridge — bridge bridge —

Tracks on opposite shores of a river.

Railway atop concrete and stone pillars   bridge stretching toward a meeting.
Of itself.

In the centre of the Skeena.

Where currents are strongest.

                                    • • •

From a road sign on Highway 16

The Skeena Crossing: Completion of this Grand Trunk Pacific Bridge in 1912 was vital to opening the Upper Skeena area. Sternwheelers, which served the camps, vanished with completion of the track laying. The rail line, which shortened the route to the Orient, was plagued by financial problems, forcing its unions with other lines in creating today's Canadian National Railway.

• • •

1911.

Black and white nitrate negative. *Construction of Grand Trunk Pacific Railway Bridge Over Skeena River.*

Snow low down on mountains. Deciduous trees barely in bud. Girders and two-by-four latticework. Shorn and scalped shorelines. Never-travelled tracks balanced   suspended. Steam engine. A crane lowering sections of bridge. Into   place.

Skeena halfway crossed.   Bridgeless   centre.

Nothing   but river   nothing but water.

The young man is dwarfed by the bridge   the crane   the river   the sky. His hand is extended.

The photo doesn't capture it   but.

Imagine.

A saucer hurled for the sheer joy of watching fine bone china. Slice air. Slice water. Launched from the grease-stained hands of a railroad engineer.

1911. A river still uncrossed by railway track.

A river still knowing the world in Skeena time.

. . .

I am the river.

I have touched

bends of sandbars
        set to disappear   tips of drifted-down pine
                needles   the husk   of a hair from a rutting bull moose   carcasses
of deer   red   red   long summer days huckleberry-full and still.

Still   you do not believe   I am small.

You refuse to believe.

Insist   I can take anything.
        Forgetting that single solitary second
of   split   water.

Of splitting me.

You   young man   are still
finishing the job.

. . .

That day   oh the day   I
became small
split halfway crossed
and railway trestles taste black taste
creosote. Black planks   black beams   blackened
nails. Built criss-cross-strong   strong   enough to shoulder the black
bulk of trains.

. . .

1926.

A.Y. Jackson completes his painting *Skeena Crossing B.C. (Gitsegyukla)*.

A small oil on canvas   measuring 53.5 by 35.9 cm   it becomes part of the
McMichael Canadian Art Collection in 1968. Blue mountains   green valleys
grey skies brushed into black.

Eleven totem poles   eastward leaning   six topped with carved birds. Ravens?
Yellow trees   three longhouses in shaggy disrepair. Four people.   A woman
it seems   standing next to a pole.

Is she walking toward the others   one standing   two seated next to the
longhouse   smoke escaping through a gash in the roof?

And what of the dog seated to the left of the man in deep orange pants?

By now the railway has been complete for fourteen years.

When trains are not running   not hurtling along young tracks
can those four hear the Skeena?

Do ravens grock grock click and craw at the pitch and whine of steam touching
nests in hemlock trees?

Do dogs howl in unison with the high-pitched wail of steel train wheels slowing
slowing   and then stopping on wet steel tracks?

Downstream.   An unpainted place.

• • •

Wet'sinkwha[1]

We join   rushing   heaving.

All of you   Wet'sinkwha

boiling into me.   Below
the Hagwilget bridge.

We join.

You into me.

. . .

<hr />

1. Together, the Skeena and Wet'sinkwha Rivers drain 60,800 square kilometres of land in northern British Columbia. The Wet'sinkwha, now known as the Bulkley, was renamed in the late nineteenth century after an American engineer in charge of the area's telegraph line.

From a road sign near Old Hazelton

Hagwilget: "The home of the quiet people" was a Carrier Indian village on the banks below. Here a bridge spanned the Bulkley River before the non-Indians arrived. Poles, lashed with cedar "rope" were supporting timbers for this noted "marvel of primitive engineering." Later, reinforced with wire by the crews of the telegraph line, it served for half a century.

. . .

Who chose to name people?   Who chose?   The people?

...

Our direction south
        south   south   and then southwest.

Always toward an estuary.   Toward
Pacific's Dixon Entrance.

We pour ourselves through Eleanor Passage.

Our reaches   human reached.

Yellow mesh wire steel scaled
scaling cliffs.

Half a century
         or yesterday morning.

Early spring.

Oh May!

Dropping seeds
invertebrate taste   breaking   our slough surfaces
our back eddies   slow sluggish bracken

waters   beyond the rush
mayflies rupture surface dimpled.

Ephemeral ephemeroptera.   Sticky transparent
wings wet   with our waters   surface   eruptions
    in our north.

In our reaches.

By the time   I reach you   Wet'sinkwha
      I have   nearly forgotten
the Klappan Valley.

Separating   from Stikine
    from Nass   from our headwaters

where the human   names   sound

like spitting

on rock
on dirt.

Spatsizi.
        Edziza.
                Tatlatui
I gather   tributaries   into watersheds

Duti   Mosque   Sicintine   Babine.

The Kispiox   under   shadows of Mount Weber.

Then you   Wet'sinkwha.

South of Kispiox   below.

• • •

From the *Cariboo Sentinel*, July 19, 1866:

Western Union Telegraph — The telegraph line is now completed to Fraser Lake, and the chopping party are some way ahead. The work is being pushed on vigorously and it is expected the line will be stretched to Rocher de Boriller, on the Skeena, by the 1st of August. Parties are exploring the Skeena River, and it is hoped the Stickeen can be crossed a short distance from the coast. Over 250 pack animals are employed transporting wire and supplies. About 100 pack animals and the same number of beef cattle left Quesnel mouth on the 4th [headed for] Fraser Lake. The boats already made two trips to Forts Fraser and Stuart.

• • •

The highway beside us
                    again and always.

After   millennia   of days.

Once   the loudest sound
we are now   drowned out
by the CNR line.

Curve. Rail. Steel. Nail. Creosote. Trestle.

Boys on boxcars   photograph us.

Look up.

See sky.

        Snow-filled fissures fingering down hills
into waterfalls.   Somewhere west

of John Little Falls   boys of the Lordco Cosco and All Cargo Express freight
containers look up   caboose face orange   sparks flying
engines muscling and straining.

Panting.   Great sooty black breath.   Hauling.

In the end   nothing will remain
        but a greasy   creosoted   slide-trail.

                        · · ·

From *Avalanche Accidents in Canada III: A Selection of Case Histories, 1978–1984*, by the National Research Council of Canada, Institute for Research in Construction (Ottawa, 1987):

The Canadian National Railway and Highway 16 cross numerous avalanche paths between Terrace and Prince Rupert, British Columbia. Avalanches frequently cover the railway track and highway, interrupting traffic several times each winter. The accident on 12 January 1982 occurred at Railway Mile 43.5, Skeena Subdivision west of Terrace, in avalanche path No. 69.6 known as "Rockface."

ACCIDENT SUMMARY: Railway employees were repairing tracks damaged by removal of previous avalanche snow when another avalanche struck at 15:45 h. On a warning shout from the watchman the workmen ran for cover, but four men and four vehicles were caught. The powder component of the avalanche blew two men across the adjacent highway onto the river ice. A third man was thrown across the highway only and remained on the surface. The fourth one was flung under a 31.4 ton truck, which was also displaced by the avalanche and partially buried.

· · ·

Then again May.   Morning.
Cloudless sky.   Sky.

Looking up: blue.

Blue blue blue blue blue blue.
Insert of white (snow). Blue   slope of white   blue   black-grey rock.
Limb of rock   blue   blue   white   black blue blue.

Cloudless sky.   Against
snow on rock
edge of rock   an arête
sloping into cirque
cirque inclined   into waterfall.

...

Near Kitwanga   great green fields.
Grazeable   grass tidal waves weaving waving
we rivers by railway and road.

Coyotes pay us no attention.
Tricksters are humans   girls   granddaughters
swallowed   a missing   a flavour.

We gulp each gash
          each cut into human skin.

Our smolt   our young salmon
our parr and grilse   silver scales   appearing
soft armour   you sockeye   you steelhead   you coho   you chum and char

you fish.

. . .

We are passing
      canneries of   the past.

North Pacific Canning Company.
Anglo–British Columbia Packing Company.

Women packed side by side by side   slicing salmon   slick in blood
boots sloshing in sleet rain and salmon guts.

Freezing hands shoving flanks
of salted sockeye into tins.

Seals   barking   begging
for the sluice dripping from Port Edward's slippery boardwalks.

. . .

From the *Victoria Daily Colonist*:

The North Pacific Cannery was built by the North Pacific Canning Company. The company was incorporated on November 28th, 1888, under the 1878 Companies Act. On November 29th, 1888, *The Daily Colonist* reported on this recently organized salmon canning company, which was to erect buildings for that purpose on the Skeena River. Early in 1889 John Carthew, who was lauded as a very experienced and successful canner, travelled north with a cargo of lumber to the Skeena on board the *Barbara Boscowitz*. This cannery, built 6 kilometres south of Port Edward in 1889 was the North Pacific Cannery.

. . .

One hundred years later.

Port Ed   all rotting
    wharves   piers   piercing me
pylons   barnacles   blue-black
    mussels   ghost nets   and rusting machines.

We at the Pacific.

Taste of salt   brine
flung open.

Burn of chuck
tidal line
stained rocks.

Wave eaten.

. . .

From a road sign outside Port Edward:

Inverness Cannery. The developing provincial salmon fishing industry spread northward when the Inverness Cannery opened here in 1876. The first cannery in northern British Columbia, it took advantage of the abundant sockeye runs up the Skeena River to challenge the dominance of the canneries along the lower Fraser. Closed finally in 1950, the plant was destroyed by fire in 1973.

• • •

Gitenmax. By Charles Horetyzky, 1872. PA#9162. Courtesy The Bill Reid Centre for Northwest Coast Studies.

Gitanmaax

From the Bill Reid Centre for Northwest Coast Art Studies,
Simon Fraser University:

The first settlement in the region was several miles away at the village of
Temlaham. This large community was subsequently destroyed by a
massive landslide that began on Rocher Déboulé (Stekyawden) Mountain on
the opposite side of the Skeena River. Modern geology has demonstrated that
the side of the mountain terraplaned on a cushion of air burying the town on
the opposite side of the river from the mountain. This event is now dated at approx-
imately 4,500 years ago. The devastation of the slide blocked salmon from pass-
ing this point on the Skeena River for possibly a decade or more, and forced
most of the inhabitants down the Skeena and over to other river systems
seeking subsistence. The restoration of a bountiful environment in this region
appears to have taken place two miles north of the landslide, and former village
site, on the tongue of land between the Skeena and Bulkley Rivers, which is
where Gitanmaax or Gitenmaks was a settlement that
persisted through to the time of contact.

. . .

A story.[2]

A girl   and a cloud-ground-feather-snow more-than-human   creature.

   Two sets of skins   slick as aspen saplings bark peeled back   bent touching

wet roots   hard   wooden knot   the branches windstorm   exhausted.

Then the scents   sap   lichen   mushrooms   moss   freshly slid soil.

The more-than-human creature.   Evaporates.

Downriver.   Smoke   inside a house   the high chief's house.

        His daughter's belly sprung in spring.

        Her father's fury.

Where is her creature lover?

Douse all fires   pack all canoes   abandon the daughter.
Remember a running mother.   Gift clutched.

The salmon gone too.

                . . .

_____

2. Gitanmaax translates as "People of the Torchlight Fishing Place." As far as I know, the human (as opposed to geological) story about Gitanmaax has not been written down. As I have heard it, this story centers on a powerful chief who abandons his daughter when he discovers she is pregnant through a relationship with a supernatural being. Alone and despite near-death, the daughter gives birth to three sons in the place of her abandonment — a place now cursed and bereft of salmon because of the chief's exodus. Shortly after her sons are born, the daughter is instructed, likely by her former lover, to summon the salmon by lighting strips of wood and bark along the river. In this way, she calls back the fish and is able to feed her sons. Her human family also returns to the site eventually known as Gitanmaax.

When snow reaches belly height   even moose
tread tiredly — a trailing tunnel   a scar
on winter white.   One night   the girl
called out to me —

river oh river —
I'm going to climb into you
              and freeze
  all white

. . .

Inside her   three babies   turned.   Lurched.

A tunnel trail   tiredly   womb worn.

Then   exhausted like moose in snow   they mewled to the world.

Storm born   sky rough   hailing eagle feathers.

Great wind in spruce trees.

A creature   calling   I am a father   I am your father.

Calling   a song to his sons   his human wife   a torch.

Make   long   long strips from aspen bark
take them   take them   dry them
lover mother   dry them.

The salmon will come.

Light the strips   light the strips   light
and line them   up   up along the river's banks.

The salmon will come.

Our babies will grow
into men   fat with the fish   you lover
*   you mother*
you will feed them.

The salmon will come.

. . .

So no scars   no sobbing   no graves   only
    strips of aspen   cedar kindling.

Salmon swimming   toward the light.

. . .

Winter

When horses are steaming
                    thick-furred whinnying
          for warmth
of composting hay.

Clotted manes   mud
strings   of saliva.

When you   winter
make me   wild mean.

Each   year   new

winds   end wetness   endless   grey
crushing ice a tightness

bottom boulders
slow   inching   insects
larva in my belly.

My back exposed   cool rest
awaiting   a squalling.

You descend.
     I pull back   peel away.

Sometimes you're slow.
Sometimes you're hard.

I wait and wait and wait

fatten my reserves in the highest lands.

Mt. Beirnes   Mt. McEvoy   Seven Sisters.

Even Mt. Kenny.

Once   a faint taste of frozen meat   seal
slices soft fat gone hard.

Near Usk. Just
beyond Cedarvale
a chickadee dee dee dee
     beak full of brittle high-bush cranberries
tiny   bursts   bitter winter   dried and frozen sugar.

Don't let me
steal   your bright bit of   bird.

For you winter
     I'd swallow it down whole.

. . .

From the *Bella Coola Courier*, January 18, 1913:

There is no more difficult river in the world to navigate than the Skeena. Its currents in all seasons are never the same. The captains who navigated the river fleet in its prime spent their working hours in continual fight anticipating the Skeena's latest cantrip. [Once] the spirit of the Skeena enlisted the aid of the Erl-King in the bush by the river-banks, and made effort to crush the life out of an intrepid captain and sink his boat by flinging a huge tree right down on top of it ... her decks and sheathing were crushed like the shell of an egg ... and through the splintered, gaping rents in her framework the baffled river spirit could see engines throbbing away with imperturbable efficiency ...

...

Bridges

Feet deep sunk   into my bed
girders   sand-glistened
stroked polishing   the base

I heave against your downward heft

you're drilled   bored
below the mud slick
thick you grind me   grounded.

I spit mountains
against your pilings beneath
your decks   wood steel
mesh concrete tracks iced
wheels whirring I rest gridded.

Unzipped around your foundations
like a feather pulled   unglued
                    a split
                    a split
nothing puts me back.

Trains and trucks hurling grassy globs
animal shit   tire rubber   salt   strips
swerving snakes off the 18-wheelers
still ripping they   slap me.

Wind hung fungus skunk cabbage scents
steel   meshed crossing leathery
porcupine feet cling to you

                              scuttle

                                                   scuttle
             quill-less porcupine stomach
soft as young hemlock branches.

                              ...

Riparian

I owe you   beyond   all else.

                    ...

Along with me   along me   every second   every
      fleck of watersoil   every root
my route my overstep my sides my skin my containment my breaks my ins
my outs   my edge.

...

And I will   flood you   wash you   out.

. . .

I wreck you
        take over   bloody your
burrowing bank swallows   your beavers   your beds   our curve
carved

by salmon flanks in dying
days of rot-green flesh.

A saw-whet owl
chick   resting smaller than a shrew
exhausted flying
           forest homeward

         I suck   that baby in   wet lip lick   kick.

. . .

I dream of giving
you driest white ash sun bleached
to bloom   to stay   for centuries.

Let that be.

Instead.

Our new grasses
our greenery

gone.

. . .

Again.   I flood.

...

Flood blueberry
      flood   lupines   flood deep purple   white
            slide alder   ferns   sandy spore spots

underside of leaves

rosebuds going to rosehips   spikes and spicy seeds

Indian paintbrush   Indian hellebore   fields of daisies   fireweed
yarrow and salmonberry   salal elderberry cow parsnip
dandelion   stinging nettles   buttercups   clover   and thistles.

I gag you   you retching salmon
onto moss clay and sand onto cedar bark surging wetness

beyond my banks.

I know   your   sturgeon
were never meant to swim
through spruce trees.

I know your   seals
          should never float
over rusty soft muskeg bogs.

I know your   every   pebbly grey alluvial   fan
every depositing of your sands your gravels your woody debris your side's
      offerings from high   your   your   you.

. . .

From the Royal British Columbia Museum's Living Landscapes project:

One of the first families to pre-empt land and build on the north side of the
Skeena was the Bateman family. Following their father's dream of wilderness
and entrepreneurship, the family moved from Oregon in 1905. After scouting
out several locations in the northwest, they finally built at Remo amongst the
cedar and hemlock in 1906. In a 1958 retrospective Emma Lindstrom
pondered changes [to Remo]: "the Skeena had flooded over its banks several
times ... and the old pre-emption has been logged and tractors have taken the
logs off" (Terrace Herald, 1958). The Froese family arrived in 1932. There was
no school at that time since there were too few children in Remo to justify it.
In the summer months the children from the south side would take the small
ferry across the river to school outside their community, in the winter months
they would perilously walk across the ice-covered river. In 1936, the river
flooded and jeopardized houses and buildings all along the Skeena Valley. The
[Froeses'] farm was fully flooded and the water reached halfway up the house.
Some houses were more damaged, and likely destroyed. The flood also spelled
the end of the Remo ferry, as it was swept down the swollen river and sank.

...

Gravel roads
horse paddocks
running muck
chickens loose
women clucking
limp armed.

Log cabins yarded
from dryness
hand-packed chinking
broken-down doors
drowned flowered
cotton dresses.

. . .

Yes.   I do.   Riparian.

...

Tributaries

Before we had names
                          time was ice
being gone me
          becoming   ice.

Invertebrates nuzzling   my bowels.

Light slipping to dark slipping to light
and then to dark: rutting moose.

Leaf smoke   following   lightning strikes.

My surface silky with eagle down
                          thistle fluff.

Soapberries green going red.

Splintering oolichan in heating days
          after crows finish nesting
          black feathery chicks falling accidently into me.

Before we had names   I measured
                          here and there
in salmon eggs buried thin
in flat rock   sharp stone   sand.

In the gap   between   granite
                    and   eelgrass.

In spruce cones and not salal.

In places with molluscs in places of grizzlies.

Then the names came.

Voices called over
our waters
soil markers
valleys stated.

Shilahou   Slamgeesh   Sustut.

Slippery words forced into us.

You were once
slow-and-full-of-water-with-lily-roots-thick-as-a-young-doe's-knee-knuckle.

You were soft-green-horsetails-touching.
          You.   Where-seals-nose-into-salmon.
And you?   Always-sliding-gravel-once-the-snows-lift.

Or beaver-fat-thick.
Taste of grizzly shit shot with tannin
leached through peat   orange-rust
colour marked where you
cleaved into me.

Then gold and railways
                    metal metal metal
and then   more metal and
you were no longer
waters-last-to-be-free-of-snow-and-ice-cooler-of-my-headwaters.

Boucher Creek   Comeau Creek   Cullon Creek
Deep Canoe Creek   Fulton River   Harold Price Creek.

Where did the flavour of rotting
packed-down muskeg go?

Where are traces of caribou scat
mating coyotes   and the struggles
of Dolly Varden trout on steep
shoots of thin waterfalls?

Salmon Run Creek
Sockeye Creek
Spring Creek
Star Creek
Thomas Creek

No longer
rotten-fiddleheads-frothing-churned-through-mud-flavoured-like-blood-and-
iron-into-my-open-flanks.

Nanika and Nilkitkwa
remnant river singing
names often misspoken.

Kleanza Creek.

What was wrong with
you-who-meets-me-slow
across-gravel-you-short
short-girl-who-bundles
in-deep-pools-bubbling
after-hurling-herself
over-thin-rock-lips?

. . .

Nameless by humans

     we still

                   water-fed
each other

still called.

                        ...

From "Biogeochemical Contributions to the Water Quality of the Skeena River" by Solomon Henson, 2004:

The inputs on the main stem of the Skeena River are in large part controlled by inflowing tributaries. These tributaries are fed by turbid glacial meltwater, groundwater aquifers replenished by snowmelt, or wetlands. Based on these hydrologic flowpath regimes, each basin carries its own chemical signature, and the geology of the basin determines which constituents are available for mobilization. As the Skeena River flows down through the intermontane belt, it may pick up the highly turbid flows of glacial meltwater from one source, and then be diluted by a large clean flowing snowmelt tributary from the next. The timing of the tributary contributions is an ever-present force creating strong yearly patterns in water chemistry. In the winter months the Skeena River runs clear, while the spring months are characterized by high discharge and may have high turbidity due to glacial meltwater. These yearly chemical patterns shape and interact with the biological community determining size and quality of algal, bacterial, and fish populations and providing seasonal cues for fish migration and spawning. Biotic populations add the final layer of complexity to the biogeochemical cycle of nutrients and other solutes as organisms grow, die, and degrade. The water quality of the Skeena River is intricate and highly complex, but it provides a crucial foundation for understanding how the health of the ecosystem is maintained.

. . .

Mountains

Wrinkle   crease   crumple
line   snow   stretch
marks   marking   tight fold of rock
stench of elk urine
        sliding into me
you all rut all
year long   in heat
furrow   valleys   interlocking sheep horns
     bashed   folding back
         grey bone but not.

I see you from below
from you I flow
I see you from below
from you I flow.

...

Mt. Tommy Jack — South Pass Peak — Kispiox Mountain — Howson
Range — Lonesome Crag — Polemic Peak — Mt. Glen — Seven Sisters —
Mt. Season — Bornite Range — Shelf Peak — Barrel Sides Peak — Kispiox
Mountain — Nine Mile Mountain — Thomlinson Range — Babine
Range — Slamgeesh Range — Artemis Peak — Mt. Season — Skeena
Mountains — Mt. Redemption.

. . .

Ice   above tree
line   fissures   tight broken sliced   shoots and   water
falls from clouds
onto grooves
        leather-like
            rotting hides of ungulates
                        piled skyward
                             let in the sun.
                            Let it warm me
                  you monumental carcasses
            you remains of monstrous fights
          you upended remnants
      folding earthward
earthward again.

Headless animals   rot-spotted with lichens
        in silver-orange
               now   too   you are fists all pimpled
with radio receivers.

You are cartilage   carnage   shedding velvet   glaciers
    my birth   a melt and molting.

You are all   each   and   every one   of you
wing   thieves   winds gulped gagged
back out   I watch eagles disappear
    your peaks
stealing   things of flight.

. . .

Copper³ River

We are on such familiar terms

                        locals to each other   touching

rock work   twisting radials   of ammonites.

Pressed.

You deliver to me

                a sea

                    from long before

we are us.

                   . . .

---

3. The "Copper" River is only called the Copper River by "locals" (principally settler locals). On maps and in most "formal" (e.g. not local but, rather, scientific or touristic) documents and records, the river is referred to as the Zymoetz. The Copper/Zymoetz is home to the locally famous Copper River Fossil Beds.

From "Floodplain Erosion Hazard Mapping Zymoetz (Copper) River, Terrace, B.C.," *Forest Sciences: Prince Rupert Forest Region* (August 1996):

In the early 1960s, the Copper River Forest Road was built. The road followed the river for 50 kilometres and ended north of Limonite Creek. Long sections of the road were built on the floodplain. In the early 1970s, the natural gas pipeline from Smithers to Terrace through the Telkwa Pass was also routed along the lower Zymoetz River. In November 1978, a 100-year flood eroded many sections of the road and the pipeline: some sections were abandoned, others rebuilt. Repeated flooding in 1988, 1991, and 1992 damaged and eroded many of the rebuilt road sections. What had been considered a "stable" road location for the first 15 years, now seemed to have become a chronic and expensive problem demanding long-term solutions.

. . .

Coral reefs and plankton   lace now
hemlock bows after salt
has sunk left pale spice in fossils
white crystal quartz and trace
elements   exoskeleton   sketch lines.

Running red this clay
                    episodic flooding
those beds of Jurassic
                    sleep stirring up
          sediments   wet erosion
dust thickened into muck
                         stuck against cottonwood
islands plunked in our wandering
gravel bed channels.

Braid earth skin   flat into me
                         forget aggradations
stay channel open   together we
wash away bridge after bridge ancient
tide times tying us to
each other   copper in
the veins   copper in
the waters   copper in
                         scales on summer-run
steelhead returning from the present
                         sea anadromous like you
returning to   me
from a once upon sea
now high and   dry

in the Telkwa Range.

Peaks   are   Sinemurian outcrops
            rocks at work
      again   somewhere close
to dawn   redwood remnants
coppery   red   long ago   mud   drunk.

...

Metallic prehistoric — tastes into me — we will head

seaward together
red cedars

new saline soils.

. . .

Raven

Is it true
      great big black bird

that nothing in this world

surprises you anymore?

Nothing

shocks or stuns or stops you

in your winging turning tracks?

Certainly nothing
      not even a river like me
compares to your work.

Of making the world.

Of shattering stars into
oceans blue as mourning.

Of pulling humans from clamshells.

Of being   argillite-feathered beast
             abalone gleam trickster shifter.

Not even red cedars turning
silver with my waters
hold the element of surprise.

But what of this?

A place of   collecting concretions.

A place of   small and heavy
black bite-sized chunks
smooth and weighty
humans collect them. Roll   and   turn them
in their human hands.

Big black bird
I will name it for you.

Will gladly give
        it to you   if I could finally
        surprise you
trick you track you

                        spin you
                                around in flight.

                        . . .

Moon

I could confuse you

with a single vertebrate
washed ashore years after
the chum salmon rotted away

with the rain-bleached
knucklebone of a drowned
squirrel rotted to my bottom

with the orb of milky white
guts from a freshwater mollusc
black shell shattered
opened by an eagle's beak

with arêtes full
of dimpled glaciers
pockmarked melting

with an agate barely opaque
a snowflake
a strip of marrow-hued
bear claw   ripped off
during a fight of fur and screams
or the downy belly
of a trumpeter swan
amongst blocks of ice
floating above
when I face the night.

...

Moose

Early spring   overflow
                   low down with salt
near Pacific I am
devil's club just opening
    memories of aspen leaves
alder-leaf rot from last fall
beaver-fat-brown and full throttle
I'm going
    strong

all slick in the bank
I hug stumps   hurl
them sideways
huge   I love my great big spring
    self when

you tumble into me
I suckbackgasp (splooshthluck)

like a birth   spat wet into the world
you kick   bray   moose-screeching
head back eyes rolled slick snot from fear muzzle
        down to dewlap drenched   ribs heaving.

I'm going
        strong
not even you   strong enough
to climb out of me you're shitting streams
        not pellets   this is death up close
a clackcluck calling   your calf running downriver

your snapped leg
        one
     two
  all four
bash   bash   bashed against a root
    how hale your bones   how fragile in water
your still-wintery fur
downy underneath

your willow-tip breath
gone
I am in your
lungs   I am going
     strong.

• • •

The head of Kitselas Canyon, Royal BC Museum and Archives B-05847.

Kitselas (Canyon) [4]

How long have I been in you?

Between you?
        Channelled by you?
                Rocked and gutted by you?

Gorged and disgorged since before
    the Quaternary epoch   since before
the Holocene   screeching to an end
in retreating ice   a melting into me   the massive
Cordilleran stripped bare flexing

lifted up   warm winds and sun.

I am a dilute stream in your innards.
Until the day I swell.
Until the day I fill you up.

You do not yield. Do not stand
down. You do your best to empty me
gut me quick and slick   rock edges
slice-me-up   score my surface. In your cracks
I am choppy flip-flopping whirlpools   narrowed
    and deepened   canyon constricted. Your tracks
knuckle out into my midstream   granite protrusions
    sedimentary striations
hardened.

---

4. Kitselas Canyon is one of the narrowest stretches of the Skeena River. Less than two kilometres long, it was a major obstacle to steamboat travel on the Skeena in the early twentieth century. The canyon is situated east of Terrace between the community of Usk and the Tsimshian community of Kitselas.

How long I have been in you.

Since   the late Pleistocene   since before
western hemlock since before Sitka spruce
when willows wove through still warm
          soil   when alder was all I heard
                              alder-call   alder-call.
                              That first time through you
I learned the opposite of   broad lands.
The opposite of   flatlands.
Opposite of   soft glacial till   muskeg marshlands.

Learned   shearing   a chute a trench a gully
no giving no giving   way
spent   given   never   getting back.

Digested and shot out.

How long I have been in you.

We alone   remember
          the first voices.

                    Symalgyax̲.

Larynx   syntax   and lexicon
calling against the wind.

Voices and feet on ferns   voices and a village.
A rock as tool   a rock in hand.   You
are scratched and scared.   Hand put upon.

Black line scorched.

        You   Kitselas   my canyon
  my rock-hold   are fisted fingered infiltrated
and illustrated.

        Petroglyphed.

              ...

From the Kitselas Nation:

The Gitselasu — People of the Kitselas Canyon — have thrived in this territory with the abundant, fertile rivers and lands in the beautiful valley of the Skeena since "time immemorial." They continue to work and live in this rich landscape and have a very proud heritage that is still practiced today. Archaeological and ethnographic evidence suggests people have occupied the Kitselas Canyon area for at least 5,000 years. The language used by the Kitselas Nation is Tsimshian (or Symalgyax̱). The coastal and inland dialects of the language differed only in the use of a few words. There are four main clans. Everyone in the Tsimshian First Nation belongs to one of the clans or sub-clans. The main clans are: Gispudwada (Killerwhale), Laxgiboo (Wolf), Laxsgiik (Eagle), Ganhada (Raven). Presently, the Kitselas membership totals approximately five hundred plus persons. The Kitselas Territory is comprised of nine reservations, three of which are occupied (the communities of Gitaus, Kulspai and Endudoon). The Kitselas are among seven Tsimshian groups who occupy Northwest BC.

. . .

The Landing Place landed upon.

Village makers.

The people grow. Family lines. Deep into
our private canyon.

Voices rise above alders.

Those with voices have marked you
Kitselas. Landed
creatures   village makers   chipping
into your unyielding hips
a rock tattoo   a mark   a memory   a never
erased scar.

Two petroglyphs
in canyoned you who
never let me go.

At first   I   churn   thrilled.
          Louder than my rushing strangle-held calls!

Longhouses   children   a story of three
young men felled by frogs   a story
of *Pelemgwae*   the giant beaver who shot arrows
and felled a chief   whose beaver wife had a human face
whose dam was broken by salmon-eaters
                    by raven   by eagle by *adaawak*.

The only storyteller
                    to hear.

Fern on fern on fern on lichen   crushed.

Copper plate   interruptions   property
markers human-palm-sized marking
lines   sap lines running down   iron slivers nailed
into torsos of Sitka spruce   blood lines   lines of forest
cleared. Sore guts. Sawdust. Landing
        on my surface   pale flecks too light   to sink
buoyant on a back eddy.

A tree frog caught in draught. Skin limp. Skeletal.

. . .

The railway trip on the G. T. P. Ry. from Prince Rupert to Skeena Crossing is full of interest. The Skeena river with its rapid waters, its canyons, tributaries, mountain scenery, small villages, stations and embryonic garden lands, is full of charm and instruction.

The railway will soon be running past Hazelton to the property of the G. T. P. Coal Co., twenty miles east of Old Hazelton. The construction of four steel bridges will see the work completed as far east from Prince Rupert as above indicated.

In fact, the province, as well as the whole Dominion will throb with a new life, and there will soon be a long line of villages, towns, cities, settlements and commercial, industrial, lumbering, farming and mining activities brought into existence. As it was with the C. P. R., so will it be with the G. T. P. This new line is of incalculable interest and value to all Canada and the British Empire. It is an important part of the present empire-building process.

Clipped from *The Western Call*, August 9th, 1912. Accessed from UBC Library's British Columbia Historical Newspapers Archive.

A man   of marks   a name whispered.
Commissioner O'Reilly. September 18, 1893.

Timber Reserve. Indian Reserve. Railroad Reserve.
Git'aws to Indian Reserve No. 1
lat 54°37' N - long 128°25' W
Tsmdimaas to Chimdimash Indian Reserve No. 2
lat 54°41' N - long 128°21' W
Endudoon to Kshish Indian Reserve No. 4
lat 54°34' N - long 128°28' W

• • •

From *The Great Canadian Rivers Project*, "The Skeena River":

Small steamboats appeared briefly on the turbulent Skeena from 1864–1866, hauling supplies for the ill-fated Collins Overland Telegraph. When a transatlantic cable put an end to the ambitious North America-to-Siberia project, the steamboats were retired. Fifteen years later, in 1891, the Hudson's Bay Company launched a specially commissioned Skeena sternwheeler known as the *Caledonia*. At one hundred feet in length, she was judged too short to handle well and was returned to the Victoria shipyards to be lengthened. During the next two decades, the company operated a succession of sternwheelers between Port Essington and Hazelton, often competing fiercely with private entrepreneurs such as Robert Cunningham, who launched the *Hazelton* in 1901. Skeena riverboating had become a lucrative business, serving the traders, prospectors, merchants, and missionaries that briefly transformed Hazelton into the largest community in northwestern British Columbia.

...

In you   Kitselas   I lose
     my memory.   I forget many things.

How long we have been together   Kitselas.
How long   oh how long

have I been in you?

                              . . .

Rain

Me   in   me   in   me   in   me   in
        me   in   me in me
t-t-t   me
in me   t-t-t-t-ppsh-t-t-t-t-t-t
     in   me   in me.

I
     taste
          falling
p…ppp…ss……ss………ht………t-t-t-t-t-t………… — you —

up-air
     then down

          t-t-t-t-ppssssssttt-t-t-t-t-t
onto me.

You are high — velocity rich   air   born   salty drops — s —

cedar sap scented
pinprick   pointed
     puncture   surface tension
     p……p……ps……s……ssh……hhhhttt-t-t-t-t-t-t-t-t-t-t-t-t…
          cloud break.

I evaporate   you   shed you slough you brightness shuttering
          t-t-t-t-pssshhhh-t
you slip on city streets   swirl down granite ledges   tap on glass

You take me and return. Tangy.

I swallow me in me in me
t —   t —   t —   t —   p —   p —   p —   p —   p…
…sssssssssshhhhhhhttt… … … …. …t —   t —
Tomorrow I will touch skyscrapers!
Boreal forests!
Steam   from a black bear's back   hot from running.

Blinking t-t-t-t-t-t
glinting splinters.

You balance me
on stinging nettles
thorax of dragonflies
each part of you smaller
than the bubble of oxygen
aquatic beetles balance
beneath their abdomens.

                    Fall down
                        sweet.
                    Fall down
                        long.
                    Fall down
                        short.
                        Fall
                 ppsshhh-t-t-t

                        • • •

Ali[5]

Stroke.　　Current.　　　　　Current　　　　stroke.
Muscle. Thin film of flesh. You.

Stroke　　current. Me. Stroke　　　　　　current.

Ripple run my river rapids
parted　　　　a back stroke　　a resting
turning sideways then face
downwards front crawl.

Stroke　　　　　muscle　　　　stroke　　　　current.

You are a dollop　a moving
droplet　　　　the texture of freshwater
molluscs stripped of shell　　　jelly soft
silvery slippery　　　　　sand in your folds
hair fanning through me.

Your skin membrane　　　　　a watery system
veins like tributaries　　thin splinters and blue
sparks. I brush up against
　　　　the estuary of your heart　　　　aortas
draining into salty rush
oxygen uptake　　　breathing from the side
　of your mouth　　　　　red blood cells
like salmon roe. Riparian ribs. Swim me
swim me　　your body seal-slick
you take me in your mouth

---

5. In the summer of 2009, thirty-three-year-old Ali Howard, a chef living in Smithers, BC, swam the length of the Skeena River to raise awareness about the uniqueness of the river's ecosystem, including the river's salmon runs.

exhale. Stroke. Inhale above
my surface   turn   stroke   muscle
water   stroke.

. . .

From letters written to Ali by school-aged children to whom she spoke about swimming the river:

Dear Ali. Dear Ali. Dear Ali.
Thank you. Thank you.
Thank you.

You are so brave.
You are a great swimmer.

Thank you.

Thank you for helping our fish. I love to eat boiled salmon.
You must be so happy because you got to see so many fish.
I love fishing and eating and your last name is the same as mine.

Thank you.

You are so brave to have swum the Skeena.

Thank you.

Dear Ali.

· · ·

What a bundle
of tastes you are Ali!

White clover flavoured
autumn grasses drying ocher
decomposing cattails   exploded seeds
the tang of a slate quarry   your pores
the rattle of milkweed crumpling
beneath the first snow.

That half a glass of white
wine you didn't quite
finish last night before diving
into me this morning.

Like a young
porpoise   but where do you go
after dark?   Leave me   dripping
on to land and out of touch.

The curve of your spine
skeleton structured you in
boneless me   your sweat strength
swimming me
swim me.

311 km down me in me   you
turn   back flip   back slide   slip
          a somersault   suspended swimming.

. . .

From *Birds and Mammals of the Skeena River Region of Northern British Columbia*, by Harry S. Swarth, 1924:

Results of this classification of the birds by their zonal predilections may be summarized as follows: that the valleys of the upper Skeena region, east of the coast ranges, are in the Canadian Life Zone; that on the surrounding mountains there is a well defined belt of Hudsonian Zone; and that the treeless mountain tops pertain to the Alpine-Arctic Zone. At this latitude the Canadian Life Zone does not reach the coast, where but two life zones can be defined, Hudsonian from sea level upward to the tree limit, and Alpine-Arctic above that.

. . .

American Dipper

Not   bird of prey
                        or long-legged wader
neither   talon nor
            mud-sunken-in shore patience

you are   a swimming song
bird   pebble to boulder hopping

dip dip bob bob bob dip
body down   diving.

· · ·

With nothing but the thinnest see-through
nylon line knotted tight   right
around your neck   I first take
notice of you in 1959.

Why did you venture
to me   dip dip bob bob
from some smaller
stream   bubbles cold?

Fly-fishing flung itself upon
me fsst fsst fsst the flicking of fishing
line and flies fur and feathers glued
to metal twisted into Js   a finch's
beak   barbed hooks
invisible 40-pound-test
zipping over my surface
wet skimming I watch
human wrists   wondering.

Where were you
before I noticed?

Rare.

Because you're faster under
and through clear water.

I'm too turbid.

You're from stream zones.

You're heavier than silt.
Lighter than stone.

Sized like the tail
of a large chinook salmon
coloured like that salmon's deepest
dots grey-blue shot with pewter
in just the right light.

Zeet zeeeeet zeet   dip
dip bob bob   zeet   song sucked
back with breath held
tucked wings   arrow tight
eyes wide open
some insect
some stray floating
salmon egg swallowed
wing through me.

Before nylon you
swam   singing into snags
snacking on the odd smolt without
worry about what pound-test
waited to be wound
around your singing throat.

Then I noticed.
You.
Swimming songbird.

. . .

Zymagotitz, Exstew, Kasiks, Exchamsiks[6]

My brothers
            slow   four green-eyed men.

Siblings running   from our motherlands.
                Once children   of high-ice   Khutzeymateen.

I am your lowlands.

The depression   you fall to   the place you go
when there is no place left.   When you are downward bound.
                            I am the family member you can't
ignore. A liquidy topographic pull
an ocean outlet
with tides and gravity on my side.

You are sandy   bottomed   and silt
    sloped fancy dressed in cliffs
in slides and gullies   in salmonberry bushes and devil's club
in hemlocks and snapped-off cedars   in blowdown and mountain
goats chased by black bears   in just-hatched owls and side sloughs
in alders and avalanches   in waterfalls and ferns in willow trees
and a single scream of a two-day-old moose with a broken leg
taken down by a timber wolf a thousand years ago.

Come on down   down to your lowland love.

There's no place   else for you to run.

---

6. The Zymagotitz, Exstew, Kasiks, and Exchamsiks are four adjacent tributaries of the Skeena.

Fat-waisted Zymagotitz   you are first
to join us.   The clumsy   one   thick
        limbed   awkward   graceless   adolescent
boy.   All ejaculate and fawning gushes
coho in your mouth jammed with debris
backwaters   sweetening your taste
your barely contained foams.

And you Exstew   prettiest of the four.
You preen   take your green   most seriously.
Deliver   it to me   rejoicing.   Dotted
with red canoes   with humans   who fawn   pluck up
            autumn chanterelles pushed up like ornaments.
Sea lions call to you   gold-glinting cottonwood
leaves lingering on your surface. Child of your mother
                              stench of grizzly still stuck to you.

Is it true Kasiks   your sands taste sweet?
Your back eddies   enthrall me   I marvel at your slow   slow running
into me.   Seducer   middleman.   Confident child.   Not quite trusted.
You hoard ice shards in winter   collude
flood easily   refuse me   cool in summer
        calling chinook salmon and seals   the first blades
of eelgrass and ripe elderberries.
That petroglyph   just west
            of your mouth   a face smiling through lichen   even I
do not understand.

            Oh   Exchamsiks   you come last.
        Fretting shaking   smaller
thinner   always playing catch-up   a millennium
of never winning.   Greenest of all
                        with the gentlest touch.
    Sometimes you fool me. Make me   believe   you're *choosing* me above

clouds   the coveting rain   coaxing   roots of yellow
          cedar. Like you said no   to those glaciers
and nosed into me.   You sibling on the run

making me feel wanted
brother of my lowest lowlands.

· · ·

You are my ending.

. . .

My gone   to salt   my turned   to rockfish my
                                  orcas ripping into dogs my belly of oolichans

my eagles shot   feet cut off   my waters seared
with red tide   my lost abalone   my chainsaw grease
and clearcut sawdust   my otters drowned
my hills underwater melting with kelp   my greens
going grey into black   my train tracks

my throat.

I pass it all along to you.

I give you the girl who swam me   every
inch of her   stroking

I give you   the highway I tore at
                    flecks of yellow that never sank.

I give you moths that fell   into me
        their wings collapsed   bright with exhaustion.

. . .

I give it all to you.

I give it all to you.

. . .

ACKNOWLEDGEMENTS

Sincere thanks to editors of journals and texts who have, over the years, published sections of *Skeena*: *ARC Poetry Magazine; Spiral Orb: An Experiment in Permaculture Poetics; The Goose: A Journal of Arts, Environment, and Culture in Canada;* and *Make It True: Poetry from Cascadia.*

With thanks to the Piper's Frith Writing Retreat at the Kilmory Resort in Newfoundland, especially organizer Leslie Vryenhoek and poetry mentor Don McKay – who early on gave astute guidance about writing *Skeena*.

Thank you also to the incredible team that is Caitlin Press: Vici Johnstone, Andrea Routley, Kathleen Fraser, and Benjamin Dunfield.

Skeena would not be half the book it is without the outstanding editorial work of Patricia Young — an intelligent, witty, insightful, and patient woman from whom I've learned a great deal about writing poetry. Thank you.

Unquestionably, I remain indebted to Mary de Leeuw and Briar Craig. Always.

SARAH DE LEEUW is the author of five literary books and co-editor of two academic texts. She is the winner of the 2013 Dorothy Livesay Poetry Prize, a two-time recipient of a CBC Literary Award for creative non-fiction and, in 2014, won a Western Magazine Gold Award for the best article published that year in British Columbia. With a Ph.D. in geography, de Leeuw works in a faculty of medicine where she teaches and undertakes research on medical humanities and health inequalities. Her creative and academic work has been widely anthologized and appears in journals from *CV2* and *PRISM International* to the *Canadian Geographer* and *Emotion, Space and Society*. Having grown up and spent most of her life in Northern BC, including Haida Gwaii and Terrace, she now divides her time between Prince George and Kelowna.

This book is set in Arno Pro, designed by Robert Slimbach.
The text was typeset by Vici Johnstone.
Caitlin Press, fall 2015.